COLLEEN ANN NORMAN has lived and worked as a teacher internation-
ally. She is the author of *A Comparison of Public Support for Moderate and
Extreme Terrorism* and *Public and First Responder Knowledge of Chemical
Nerve Agents*. Colleen graduated from the University of Liverpool with
a master's degree in Forensic Psychology and Criminal Investigation. She
is a forensic psychology practitioner who runs a consulting and psychometric company in Toronto, Canada, and is working on several children's
books and a PhD proposal.

MI5, TERRORISM AND THE FRENCH CONNECTION

COLLEEN NORMAN

ISBN-13: 978-0-578-85651-3 (*paperback*)

TABLE OF
CONTENTS

I would like to acknowledge the late Dr. Michael Persinger, Aso Anwar, and MI5.

LIST OF
PHOTOS

Photo 1: Hyundai Beach

Photo 2: Shark diving

Photo 3: Beondegi

Photo 4: Pocheon pottery restaurant

Photo 5: Pocheon pottery

Photo 6: FIFA World Cup

Photo 7: Kyoto

Photo 8: Kyoto

Photo 9: Eurocopter

Photo 10: Colleen flying

Photo 11: Sumo wrestlers

Photo 12: Mainoumi Shuhei

Photo 13: Parisian artist

Photo 14: The Palais

Photo 15: Arc du Triomphe

Photo 16: Near Le Louvre

Photo 17: Passports

Photo 18: 800 military added to Skype

Photo 19: DMZ

CHAPTER ONE
MYSTERIES

W HAT MAKES A mystery alluring to you? Is it the twists and turns, or is it the unknown? Mysteries are mentally engaging in a way that other genres of writing are not. Mysteries require us to use our cognitive abilities to interpret the clues as well as our imagination to identify with the characters in a true crime story. There is also an element of intrigue. The unknown or uncertainty captures our interest on a deeper level. Mysteries engage us emotionally, pique our curiosity, offer elements of surprise, interest, anger, doubt, disgust, and other affective states. They challenge us to use reason, logic, and deduction. Hard-to-decipher clues may be impossible to figure out, and the mystery eludes us. Disappointment sets in when we fail to find the answers, and we are motivated to continue looking for clues to solve the mystery. When our deductions are confirmed, it is a rewarding experience because we have solved the unknown. It is like an epiphany! (Monaghan, 2020).

A detective once said to me, "If you only knew who was walking behind you, you would spend the rest of your life looking over your shoulders." That statement stuck with me throughout my travels around the world. I didn't worry so much about the people who were walking behind me but more about those who were around me. I would later change the detective's statement: "If you only knew who was around you, you would spend the rest of your life looking right in front of you!" Are people who they appear to be? Do we ever really know someone? We take people for granted, at face value, when we meet them and believe that they are who they tell us they are. Are we too trusting? There are some people who are natural-born predators.

Stalkers are natural born-predators. There are two stalking typologies that I feel fit the characters in this true account: one is a delusional psychotic and the other a sadistic stalker. There is also behavioral overlap between the two categories. As the story evolves, you will be able to see the established patterns of behavior that I have highlighted. Some of the behaviors of a delusional psychotic stalker are victim-fixated, incessant phone calls, emails, and visits. They may have borderline personality disorder or episodic schizophrenia. The sadistic stalker displays a progressive escalation of control over their victim financially, professionally, socially, historically, and physically. Stalkers try to dig up information on their victim's past and use it against them. They try to control the victim through fear, loss of privacy, isolation, and by undermining their self-esteem. This stalker is highly dangerous and often revisits their victim after a hiatus. It is important to note that forensic studies have found that personality disorder, high criminal versatility, and past offending are significantly related to recurrent stalking. Psychosis is the strongest predictor for increased duration. Delusional beliefs are associated with increased stalking persistence, especially among acquaintance stalkers.

The predatory nature of the two stalkers is visible throughout the book. It is as though both stalkers were hunting together. When one appeared in my life, within two weeks the second one would appear. There was a hiatus and then both reappeared at the same time repeatedly over a sixteen-year period.

PREDATORS AMONGST US

A PERSON CAN be a psychopath and go through life appearing normal to others, not even knowing that they have a personality disorder. Even if they are tested, they may score low on psychometric tests for psychopathology. They may have no criminal history, may have high grades in school, may be married and have children, may be business owners, and are often pillars of the community. An example of such a person is the Vegas Shooter.

The Las Vegas shooter was a successful businessman who was highly regarded by many. People who knew him described him as charming, outgoing, helpful, and likeable. How did he go from being a charming and engaging professional businessman to America's most notorious lone gunman? Sixty-four- year-old Stephen Paddock had meticulously planned an outrageous attack on Americans. On October 1, 2017, he callously killed sixty people and wounded 411 others before committing suicide. To date, the motive for Paddock's mass shooting is still a mystery. Paddock and his brother were not raised around their psychopathic bank robber father and didn't know about him until later in their lives. We can conclude that there was little environmental influence from the father. Interestingly, Paddock's brother also has a criminal history, and this tells us there may be a strong genetic component for psychopathology and criminality.

Psychopaths walk amongst us and are capable of criminal versatility. They lie pathologically, brag about their crimes, are highly manipulative, lack remorse, and use threats and violence to control every aspect of their victims' lives. Then to add insult to injury, they lay blame on their victims for their behavior. "Psychopathic violence is more likely to be predatory in nature, motivated by readily identifiable goals, and are carried out in a callous, calculated manner without the emotional context that usually characterizes the violence of other offenders" (Hare 2003, p.136).

A psychopath's game is great fun. Whether they are physically stalking, cyberstalking, or both, it is a game of cat and mouse. When I was a child, I recall watching in horror as my pet cat taunted a little mouse for ten minutes. The mouse would squeak and jump up at the cat, and in turn the cat would swipe at the mouse and pounce on it. The cat let it go and would wait for it to move again and continue doing the same thing over and over. It terrorized the mouse. Its eyes were bulging from its head and its tiny body was quivering with fear as it defended itself. I tried to break up the little game, but the mouse was immediately killed and devoured by the cat.

It is the same game for predatory stalkers, who instill fear, taunt, terrorize, drive their victims to suicide, or kill them in 2 percent of cases. They often promote suicidal ideology verbally or through their stalking behavior. Verbally, the psychopath will attack you on every level. They will belittle and degrade their victim in ways a normal person could not imagine. Stalkers may move things in your home, harass, taunt you with the crimes they committed against you, and try to make you feel helpless or drive you out of your mind. They may disable brake cables, create a natural gas explosion, or use more subtle means to cause harm. Some sadistic stalkers enjoy the attention and taunt their victims, families, and police. After all, the burden of proof is on the police, and the stalkers feel that they are invincible. Ted Bundy is an excellent example of a sadistic stalker.

CYBERSTALKING

CYBERSTALKING IS A highly specialized form of stalking which involves the use of information and communication technologies as the means and the medium of intimidation, threat, and harassment. A Canadian survey from 2018 showed that 28 percent of stalking victims reported being stalked on social media, which indicates that modern-day stalkers are evolving with of the advent of technology. Stalkers challenge themselves to find new methodologies to terrorize and torment their victims while going undetected. They insert themselves in people's lives by committing fraud and identity theft, threatening, stealing emails, and harassing family and friends. Stalkers use intimidation, humiliation, denigration, and exclusion to affect their victims via the Internet, and may even recruit their friends to join in their fun. This is called cause stalking or group stalking. After all, stalkers remain elusive and anonymous behind a keyboard, and few are prosecuted. They seem to have more rights than the victim when in fact stalking is a violation of the fundamental human right to life, liberty, and security and can represent serious interference with the victim's privacy and daily life. Only one in five cyberstalkers is prosecuted.

Cyberstalkers cause serious damage to their victims, resulting in sleep disorders, eating disorders, high levels of stress, feelings of being controlled, and a loss of personal safety. Victims may feel that no one will believe them; they may feel shame, anxious, depressed, suicidal, and suffer from the effects of post-traumatic stress disorder. Now imagine the damage two persons with episodic schizophrenic and antisocial personality disorder could inflict on their victims using traditional methods of stalking, in conjunction with cyberstalking.

Cyberstalking creates a challenge for law enforcement because police often lack awareness and expertise. Additionally, cyberstalking is not always recognized as a criminal offense. A lack of training or expertise to recognize the seriousness of cyberstalking can lead law enforcement to underestimate the magnitude of this crime on the victims. It becomes even more of a challenge with the global reach of the Internet. To be more specific, if a cyberstalker from Japan is committing crimes in the United Kingdom, it is difficult to obtain assistance from foreign agencies to prosecute. There is a problem with jurisdictional laws which require extradition from one region to another. Police would also have to prove that the perpetrator is the one doing the damage to the victim and needs to be caught red-handed.

There are many ways for cyberstalkers to hide behind their computers, which makes it almost impossible for a victim to make an application for a protective order. Finally, in many instances, police do not take cyber-stalking seriously and have a laissez-faire attitude. One of the two persons stalking and hacking me would type across my browser and ask: "Getting paranoid?" And they would set up email addresses similar to mine. For instance, if my email address was cnorm2000@gmail.com, they would add an extra zero (cnorm20000@gmail.com) and write to people I knew to obtain information about my whereabouts and to harass friends or colleagues. Try getting police to take that seriously and prosecute someone thousands of miles away.

Each character in this true account played a role in the mysterious things that happened in my life. You are the detective and I leave it up to you to decide which character or characters you believe are responsible for the majority of the crimes committed. The URL for the evidentiary links can be found at the back of the book. For legal reasons, I cannot put up all of the evidence such as videotapes of the suspects or full names. Can you figure out who the culprits are? Are they psychopaths, terrorists, police, military, former employers, coworkers, or an unknown entity?

Read about the measures I took to protect myself, my family, as well as those around me. As you read through the book, think about these questions: What would you have done differently if anything? Would you have taken revenge on the people involved in the crimes?

This book is written as a timeline of events highlighting approximately 10 percent of the crimes committed against myself, my daughter, a dozen teachers, as well as countless victims. The focus is not solely on crimes but other experiences as well while I traveled the world. The most important lesson to be learned from this book is to follow your gut instinct. If something doesn't feel right, it's because it's not. I hope to raise awareness and educate those who may have the misfortune of meeting suspected psy-chopaths.

It is of paramount importance to highlight the void in stalking and cyberstalking laws, police bias, and the laissez-faire police culture. The financial toll on the victims was extraordinary, and the psychological and physiological effects were devastating. How do you move forward with your life when the same people continuously wreak havoc in it and police still fail to investigate despite an abundance of evidence?

Come along with me on a compelling, shocking, thrilling, and potentially explosive adventure that took place over fifteen years, in Canada, South Korea, North Korea (DMZ), Japan, France, and the United Kingdom. This true account included twenty-two police forces, the FBI, the regional director of security for Asia Pacific, three embassies, the United States military, the Korean military, MI5, millionaires, and a psychopath or two. The crime spree by certain individuals included stalking, cyber-stalking, extortion attempts, terrorism, hacking and cracking, breaking and entering, theft, fraud, threats, damage to property, theft of intellectual property, assault, assault causing bodily harm, psychological torture, criminal harassment, and two possible murder attempts. Once again, it is your job to examine the facts and determine who is guilty of the crimes committed.

CHAPTER TWO

THE IRISH AND IMBAS
FOROSNAI

THE CELTS BELIEVE in an innate skill called *imbas forosnai* or second sight. Il imbas means *inspiration,* and forosnai means *illuminates,* and the literal translation is *wisdom that illuminates.* Some people are born with a gift for visualizing the future. Sometimes they visualize objects and other times they see a short video clip in their mind. Other terms used to describe the gifted are *seer* or *visionary.* The Celts believe that we inherit the gift of imbas forosnai from our forefathers. In my humble opinion, imbas forosnai is our seventh sense. Our sixth sense is our basic instinct, and our seventh sense is the visualization of what our sixth sense is telling us at an unconscious level in conjunction with our conscious thought processes.

Does a criminal profiler or forensic psychology practitioner possess imbas forosnai? False impressions created by "made to entertain" television shows and movies depict these specialists as psychics or visionaries. The fact is profilers look at clues and evidence, put together an overall picture of a suspect, and determine the risk or threat he or she poses to society and the best method of treatment or rehabilitation. There are many kinds of profiles conducted by forensic psychology practitioners. Their job encompasses a large number of overlapping disciplines which may include risk and threat assessments, psychological autopsies, crime scene analyses, analyses of behavioral patterns, as well as geoprofiling.

SECOND SIGHT OR LOGIC?

AT AGE NINETEEN, I worked as a fitness instructor at Lady Fitness in Toronto. I was sitting at the breakfast table with my Aunt Linda and Uncle Jack, and we'd just listened to a media report. Sharin Morningstar

Keenan, a nine-year-old, had been reported missing. The reporter stated that her neighbor had suddenly moved away and police were looking for him. I looked at Uncle Jack and said "The police will find her body stuffed in a refrigerator at her neighbor's apartment." My uncle started to laugh and said, "Yeah, right. What do you know?" The next day on the news, Sharin Morningstar Keenan was found stuffed in a refrigerator in her missing neighbor's apartment.

That afternoon, my aunt and uncle were looking at me like I had two heads. "How did you know that she would be found stuffed in a refrigerator?" Uncle Jack asked.

"It is logical," I replied. "The news report stated Keenan's neighbor had moved away. In a high percentage of cases someone known to the victim or who lives close to the victim is the perpetrator. The neighbor went missing at about the same time Sharin Morningstar Keenan did. Where would you conceal a body? Where would you hide it to slow down the rate of decomposition? In the refrigerator. Think like a criminal and everything else becomes logical." My uncle looked at me suspiciously. "I have an alibi and was working a nine hour shift at the fitness center," I laughed. This was the beginning of my career although it would take many years before I entered the field of forensic psychology.

Over the years I profiled serial killers, child murderers, and terrorist organizations, and studied the behavioral patterns of as many criminals as possible. Media accounts provided the most useful information, and police were aware that I had a hypothesis in the Holmolka-Bernardo case. Holmolka-Bernardo were the infamous Canadian serial killers who raped and murdered three young women, including Holmolka's younger sister Tammy-before they were caught. I believed a woman was involved because Kristen French's head had been shaved. My hypothesis was that a man usually cuts a woman's hair to take away her femininity. One could conclude that because French's head had been shaved, a female subject was involved. Holmolka might have wanted to degrade and humiliate French by taking away both her femininity and beauty. Holmolka's motivation would be jealousy. The second reason for shaving her head would be to conceal DNA evidence. My past successes at profiling have led to my own hypotheses about abduction styles, female accomplices, and the behavioral patterns of suspects. It is possible to profile a killer right down to what he or she looks like and wears in some instances.

Today, I work as a consultant psychologist-psychometrician and run my own company in Toronto, Canada. I have taken the opportunity to study hundreds of courses and trained with the most experienced forensic psychiatrists and forensic psychologists. The expert training has given me greater insight and understanding of various personality disorders and mental illnesses. At no time have I worked with police on any case; however, profiling is one of my passions, and I have been consulted by several people about missing persons.

THE FORENSIC PSYCHIATRIST

IN 1999, I was at the Hilton Toronto Conference Centre and Spa Hotel waiting for my coworkers to come downstairs. I was sitting on a stool at the bar when an older gentleman with snow white hair, a white beard, and a black suit walked up to me. He held out his hand and introduced himself as forensic psychiatrist Dr. Eaton Bas. "Hello, Dr. Bas. My name is Colleen," I said.

"Colleen? Ah, a shy colleen (*girl* in Irish). You are Irish, as am I," he exclaimed. "Are you here for the psychiatrist convention?"

"No, I'm not. I am actually waiting for my coworkers to arrive. We are having a meeting at our corporate office."

"Mind if I sit down and talk for a while?"

"Pull up a chair, please," I said.

"What do you do?"

"I work in corporate sales."

"Oh, do you like your job?"

"No. I'd rather be doing something else."

He stopped for a moment and stared at me.

"You are a forensic psychiatrist?" I asked. "That must be one of the most interesting jobs on the planet!"

The demeanor of the psychiatrist changed, and he grinned from ear to ear. "Yes, it can be very fascinating work."

"So you work with criminals and the criminally insane? It must be dangerous work."

"Well, sometimes it can be very dangerous work."

"How do you treat your patients?"

He spoke slowly. "I believe that in order to truly understand your client, you have to become them. Get into their minds and think the way they do. Only then can you truly understand how they feel, think, and their motivation. But..." he hesitated "...it is a dangerous place to go and a hard place to come back from."

"Hmm...you and I think alike."

Just as our conversation became interesting, one of my coworkers arrived. "Colleen, are you ready to go? Bert is waiting for us outside," he interrupted.

The psychiatrist shot a dirty look in his direction. "Well, I have to go now. Good luck with your conference." He handed me his business card, Dr. Eaton Bas. His words stayed with me and later proved to be significant. He would make a reappearance in my life.

CHAPTER THREE
TERRORISM 2001

IN 2001, I made a decision to leave my position as a quality assurance specialist in Canada to go to South Korea and teach. My daughter was fifteen and I wanted her to have a worldly education, and I could not think of a better country than South Korea. I had heard nothing but good things about it from other Canadians. South Korea is home to 51.65 million people, and kimbap, kimchi, Jejudo Island, Hangul (language), and soccer. I was offered a position in Busan, so we packed up, sold our furniture, booked our plane tickets, and said good-bye to family and friends. The idea of going to a new country was exciting, but our plans were about to be thwarted for a few weeks.

It was early morning on September 11th, 2001. I woke up at 8:50 and turned on the small color television in the living room and sat on a comforter on the floor. On the screen news reporters and camera crews could be seen running here and there, and people could be heard screaming. At 8:46 a.m., American Airlines Flight 11, a Boeing 767, had crashed into the World Trade Center's North Tower, killing ninety-two people. I called to my daughter, Diana, and told her there was a terror attack underway in the United States. She came speeding out of her bedroom to see what was going on. "A terror attack?"

"Yes, pilots steer away from buildings and will land on water or in an open field, not crash into buildings." I could see a glimmer of light off in the distance; it was another airplane. At 9:03, United Airlines Flight 175, a Boeing 767, crashed into the World Trade Center's South Tower, killing sixty-five. The rest of the day we watched in horror as the media played and replayed planes crashing into the World Trade Center, people falling to their deaths, and the collapse of Towers A and B.

The phone rang just after 5 p.m. It was my agent, who advised me that all planes had been grounded and my flight would be delayed and needed to be rebooked. We were fine with the changes because neither my daughter nor I wanted to fly over the United States at that moment. Our initial flight was to take us to San Francisco and then on to Busan, South Korea. It would be several more weeks before we would set off on our journey.

Terrorism comes in many forms. It seemed that everywhere we went in the world, there was always an element of terrorism.

FLIGHT TO BUSAN

Diana and I boarded a bus bound for Toronto on September 25, 2001, checked in at the airport ticket counter, made our way through the long lines in customs, and boarded our flight to San Francisco. We didn't know what to expect when we arrived at our final destination in Busan, South Korea. It had only been two weeks since the 9/11 terror attacks, and everyone aboard the flight appeared to be nervous. The silence aboard the flight was deafening and only the occasional whisper could be heard on the plane packed full of passengers. Even as the flight attendants went by with the food carts, a hush had fallen over the plane. Some passengers held tightly to their armrests, white-knuckled, while others sat lost in thought. The images of the attacks were seared in everyone's mind as we began our descent over the Grand Canyon. Its distinctive hue of red, brown, gray, and green seemed to glow in the brightness of the sunlight as passengers silently observed its beauty.

SAN FRANCISCO

We'd arrived at the airport and had a long wait as we went through customs. No one was allowed out of the airport and it was chaotic. People were rushing all over, lost, confused, and scared. Security staff were fielding questions and directing people to their connecting flights. The tension in the air was high, and everyone seemed to be in a pervasive state of shock. It was as though they were expecting another attack to occur at any moment. Osama Bin Laden had done what no other terrorist had. He penetrated the very heart of America and left the world shell-shocked. It was evident by the chaos at the airport that it would take a long time for things to return to normal, if ever.

An eight-hour wait and we were ready to take off again. This would be the longest part of our journey over the Pacific Ocean. The heavy turbulence made sleep an impossibility as we flew through the Gulf Stream. The trip went by quickly and the nervousness and silence that we'd experienced flying over the USA had left us. The plane was quite noisy in stark contrast to our first flight. We sat beside an older Korean man and his wife. He drank quite a bit, and by the end of the flight, his eyelids drooped and we could no longer see his eyes. He was a jovial older man who spoke English well and loved to talk. Diana and I wished we had duct tape on that long flight! We landed at Incheon, waited two long hours, and boarded our final flight to Gimhae, which is on the southern tip of Korea.

GIMHAE

OUR FLIGHT LANDED with a heavy thud, and we wearily disembarked and waited in the long line-up at customs, retrieved our luggage, and waited for our director to pick us up. Diana and I walked into the waiting area and saw uniformed Korean soldiers marching back and forth from one end of the airport to the other with automatic weapons over their shoulders. It was a frightening experience at first because there weren't any soldiers patrolling airports in Canada. An hour passed and finally Mr. Lee, a quiet, slender man in his early thirties, held up a sign with our names on it and walked toward us. "Are you Colleen and Diana? *Annyong haseyo.*" It was understood that he was saying hello.

"Yes." I extended my hand and shook his.

"You must be very tired. How long was the trip here?"

"Oh, about thirty-two hours and counting."

"There is a lot of traffic this evening, so it will take another two hours to get to your apartment," he said.

We grabbed our baggage and headed outside to the parking lot. Once outside, I was hit by the thick smell of pollution wafting in the air. It was nauseating. In fact the pollution was so bad, I could taste it. Most of it came from the bumper-to-bumper vehicles on the highway. Along the way we talked about the school, the other teachers, and what to expect. Two hours later we arrived at our new apartment. We looked around the large two-bedroom apartment and found something strange. There was a second toilet on the plexiglass-enclosed balcony with a full view from the streets. Did people actually use this? Why would there be a second toilet on a balcony? And there was no bathtub, only a shower. The water runs all over the floor and everything in the bathroom gets wet. Weird!

We went to sleep and woke up at 8:00 a.m. and took a walk outside. All of the buildings looked the same, so we wrote down the building number and mapped out the direction we were going. Within five minutes we found a store and went in. There was a young woman behind the counter speaking Korean to us. An older lady came out from the back of the store speaking Korean and walked up to me smiling and laughing. What happened next was quite unusual. The grandmother reached toward me and grabbed a handful of my butt and squeezed. Surprised, I didn't know what to say to her or how to react. I looked over at my daughter for help. The *halmony* (grandmother) was talking and laughing, and the younger one told her to let go in Korean. We bought breakfast and headed back to the apartment, laughing about the lady's actions, and an hour later we were met by the director and brought to the school. We found out that it was normal for older people to grab parts of your body in Korea in 2001.

A FEW THINGS TO DO

One of the very first things we did in Korea was head down to Hyundai Beach. We found the Busan Aquarium, a hidden underground gem. There are hundreds of marine animals to see, but the best thing about the aquarium is you can take a short diving lesson and swim with the sharks. The wetsuits are provided and it will cost you about 150,000 won for the dive. We were sure not to wave our arms around underwater because we didn't want to attract some unwanted giant fish attention! Oh, by the way, the sharks are fed beforehand. Cameras are not allowed under water, and as one can see from the photograph, the sharks do get up close and personal. Check that off your bucket list!

There are many Western restaurants if you're feeling a little homesick: TGI Fridays, Outback Steakhouse and others are close to the beach. Busan Jin Market is across the street from Hyundai Beach. You can find stores that are out of the ordinary. There is a big and tall men's shop. In the display window we saw an enormous pair of pants. One could fit five Korean women into each leg of those pants. Do people really come in that size? There are many varieties of food sold by street vendors. One of the unique edibles is Beondegi or silkworm larvae that is either boiled or steamed. It is a savory, fishy, and nutty flavored snack. Its outer shell is crunchy and the inside is soft and juicy. It will cost you about $2.00 for a small cup. Would you be daring enough to try it?

In Pocheon, for 30,000 won or $33.00 Canadian, you can try your hand at pottery. An experienced potter will take you through all of the steps to make your own bowl, cup, or plate. It takes about three hours and then you come back another day and pick up the glazed and baked item. The atmosphere of the quaint restaurant that houses the pottery shop is like being in your own grandmother's home. The hot fireplace, with steaming traditional Korean tea or coffee served with biscuits, will help you stay warm inside on a cold winter's day. Pocheon is over four and half hours away from Busan, but there are many places nearby to learn pottery. Nangman Pottery in Nampodong is one.

THE SCHOOL

THE SCHOOL WAS very wealthy, and there were many teachers. It was elaborately decorated and designed by the co-director. Each class had a theme, such as the sea. There was an aquarium between the outside and inside wall with real fish. Sponges, starfish, sea anemones, and other fish adorned the walls. The decor was impressive in comparison to anything you might find in Canadian schools. The kindergarten students were more than a handful, and this was the most difficult year I'd experienced in my nineteen-year teaching career. On the other hand it was the school where I learned the most. We had an excellent co-director who set the tone of excellence for the school.

There was only one computer for the teachers to use, so we would go over a footbridge to get to a PC room during lunch, to check our emails from back home. I asked my daughter where the washroom was, and she pointed to a door and started to laugh. "What's so funny?" I asked.

"Nothing," she replied.

I walked into the washroom and looked down. The toilet was missing and there was simply a hole in the floor with a chain above it. "What happened to the toilet, Diana?"

"Um...that is the toilet." She laughed again. "I am going back to the school. See you there."

Back in 2001, Koreans had a very unique sense of humor, and I recall all of the students running around poking teachers in the rectum with their index finger. It was a game called *dong chim* or *poop needle*. The male teachers got it the worst, because students would grab at their private parts. Every culture is different, and this was the humor that could be found on television back then. It was not an enjoyable experience, but kids seemed to think it was funny. Korean culture is full of toilet humor, and that is one of the reasons I've mentioned their humor in the book several times.

Korea had made it into the quarter finals of the 2002 FIFA World Cup, and my daughter went to two of the soccer matches with her friend and his father, the ambassador to the Netherlands and the Canadian ambassador to Seoul. I recall sitting in my apartment, and every single Korean was glued to the television, wearing red shirts with the slogan "Be the Reds" on them. When Korea won their match to get into the quarter finals, the sound in the neighborhood was deafening. People were rocking buses on the streets, waving flags, running everywhere, and shouting and singing *"Daehan Minguk"* (대한민국, 大韓民國) which is usually translated as "The Republic of Korea." It was a year of learning a new language, sharing new and exciting experiences, and meeting some pretty amazing people.

FIFA World Cup 2002

TERROR ATTACK

TRAGEDY STRUCK WHEN an American teacher and four Koreans were killed in a terror attack in Bangkok, Thailand, in 2002, while on vacation. The entire teaching community was left in shock and felt a great sense of loss. Our first year flew by quickly in Korea, and I decided not to renew my contract with the first academy. I accepted a contract working for another school and was looking forward to working at a high-security prison for young offenders. Our journey would start with an element of terrorism, continue for fifteen years, and end with an element of terrorism.

CHAPTER FOUR

THE NEW SCHOOL AND PRISON IN 2002

DIANA AND I moved to another apartment, and I started to work at a new school. In the morning, I would teach at a prison and work later in the afternoon, from 4 until 10 p.m., at a *hagwon*. The school was not wealthy but I liked the director's wife. She was pleasant to talk to, energetic, and seemed honest. She wore a short pixie cut and she was very slender. Whenever she would get excited about something, she would jump up and down and clap her hands. Ms. Kang would teach students in one class and I, the other. My students were interested in learning. They loved to laugh and have fun, even if they didn't understand 100 percent of the conversation. I recall one bull-legged teenage student, Lee Dong Min, trying on my daughter's high-heel chunky shoes and walking across the room. He could not speak English well but moved to Alberta, Canada, and spent his high school years there. On my way to Korea in 2006, he walked up to me at the Vancouver airport and spoke perfect English. We were on the same flight, seated across from each other. It is a small world after all! And it was a pleasant surprise.

PRISON

IT WAS A dull, dreary, rainy September day, 2002. Mr. Sim and I got into the van and headed toward the juvenile facility. Ms. Kang was very proud of her husband because she thought he was very handsome. He was tall, clean cut, and well dressed, had a distinctive jawline and chiseled features. His English was limited, and I took an instant disliking to him when he asked a question. He queried as to the social status of women in Canada by gesturing with hand movements. "Women in Canada here," he held his hand high, "or here?" He held his hand low.

"Women in Canada are here." I held my hand up high. "And men are here." I held my hand slightly below women. Mr. Sim gestured with his hand again suggesting that Korean women were of low social status within their culture. He continued to ask questions during the thirty-minute drive which took us over the Nakdonggang River enroute to Gimhae. He would frequently shake his fist at female drivers and complain about them over the next eight months.

We pulled up to a gated prison with three feet of barbed wire fencing on top of the walls. A guard sat in a small, enclosed area, and Mr. Sim showed his identification. Slowly the electronic gates clanged opened and we drove in. There were numerous buildings in a rectangular formation that surrounded the courtyard. I could see a prison worker barking orders at a group of twenty young men who were doing sit-ups and another group running around a track. They were all dressed alike in blue track suits, their heads shaved. Older married women called *ajumma* carried baskets of food on their heads, walking to another part of the prison. I was instructed by Sim to go into one of the buildings. Mr. Jung was waiting there for me.

I knocked on the door. "Come in," a man's voice resonated. I opened the door and walked into the classroom. A stern-looking middle-aged man was seated at his desk, scowling.

"Hello, I am the new teacher, Colleen."

"Oh...I was not expecting a woman!" He looked angrily at me.

"Well, here I am." After all, what more could I say? *Well, that introduction went over well,* I thought sarcastically as I walked to the front of the classroom and stood on the teaching platform.

I stood there waiting for my students. Ten minutes later, there was a knock at the door. "Come in," ordered Mr. Jung. Eighteen young offenders took their seats at their desks. One by one they introduced themselves by their English nicknames, which they had chosen themselves: Cherry, Anaconda, Hero, Jin, and Tiger to name a few. They were dressed in navy blue T-shirts and track suits, and a few had pieces of tissue sticking out of their nostrils. They sort of looked like fire-breathing dragons. Later one of the inmates explained that the prison relied on donations, and there was a limited amount of tissue. Rather than using large amounts of tissue for a cold, they would stuff pieces of it in their noses.

PRISON BREAK

I RECEIVED A phone call early one morning late September from Mrs. Kang telling me that I didn't have to go to the prison because something very serious had happened. A new inmate was transported in a few days earlier and had jumped over top of the buildings and barbed-wire fence, stolen a car, dragged a woman, and took two million won in cash. The woman had been dragged with the seat belt around her shoulder and was seriously injured. A manhunt was underway for the escapee, and all of the inmates were in lockdown. Three days later things were back to normal, but Mr. Jung was no longer in the classroom with me. There was a new teacher, and I was advised that Jung's job was in jeopardy as he was responsible for the security of the prison.

"Hello, I am Mr. Won, and I will be the new teacher in the classroom." Mr. Won was young, outgoing, open-minded, and didn't seem to mind that I was a woman. I felt a sense of relief. I had been under a microscope while I'd worked with Jung, and there was always so much tension in the classroom. In fact, one day Jung stepped outside of the classroom for about five minutes, and one of the prisoners got up and started to do a booty-dance in front of me while the rest of the inmates yelled, "Go, Tiger, go, Tiger!" I thought it was all in good fun and said nothing. It was rather weird to watch a person with a bony butt booty-dance!

The door flew open and Jung ordered the students to their seats. After class he asked me if anything had happened. "Not really. Tiger did a dance in front of the class."

"You don't like him, and he feels that you discriminate against him," Jung exclaimed.

"Why? Because I named him as the booty dancer?" At that very moment, I wanted to applaud the prisoner who got away. No more Mr. Jung. I believe he was transferred and his attitude went with him.

As Christmas came near, I felt a little homesick because there was no snow. Culture shock sets in around six months to one year of being in a foreign culture. One of my students asked what I wanted for Christmas. "Snow...and lots of it," I said.

It snowed six inches overnight, and when I arrived at work, we all went outside and had a snowball fight, then went to the classroom and drank hot chocolate. The atmosphere had changed and it was no longer a burden to work at the prison. The rest of my time spent teaching at the facility was a lot of fun. Mr. Won was very liberal and had great empathy for the young men.

I went on a tour of the prison facility and ate lunch with my students. The conditions in which inmates were housed were very different from the facilities in Canada. First, in South Korea, you are considered a juvenile up to the Korean age of twenty-two. This is your last chance for rehabilitation prior to going to an adult prison. Second, the young offenders are housed in large rooms with thick plexiglass walls. Twenty or more prisoners may sleep on the floor in one room. Dinner was very simplistic and consisted of rice, fish, watery soup, kimchi, and one other vegetable. Part of the prison was funded by the government, and there was a heavy reliance on donations. I never invaded the privacy of the inmates and didn't want to ask what crimes they'd committed, but not unlike Canada, many came from dysfunctional homes or had no home at all. There were three killers in the prison, but I never taught any of them.

PLANE CRASH OR TERRORISM?

IN APRIL OF 2002, my students at the prison reported hearing a plane crash. Flight 129 from Beijing to Gimhae crashed due to pilot error, killing 118 of 166 passengers and crew. I wonder how pilot error can occur when the plane tells you when you are too close to the terrain. The sensors will tell the pilot, "Terrain, terrain, pull up, pull up." Was it a pilot suicide attempt or pilot error? If it was a suicide attempt, it would have been another form of terrorism, pilot suicide.

Unfortunately, school owners don't always communicate well with their staff. When I arrived home one day, workmen were in my apartment without my authorization and had removed a water tank. I had just been paid and there was two million won hidden in my closet. Things had been tossed around the apartment, and it was a disaster. Further to that, I was never paid six million won in overtime for working at the prison, so I made a decision to leave my position four months early. Although I went to the Korean labor office and I was told I was within my right to file a claim, the owner failed to pay. There were no laws forcing school owners to pay wages back then. There is corruption in many cultures, and foreigners are often taken advantage of. I took the higher ground and left on good terms because I didn't want to create problems and found another teacher to take over for me. He was aware of the reasons I was leaving.

CHAPTER FIVE
LEAVING KOREA

I'D ENDED MY contract and my daughter asked if we could move to Japan because she had friends in Tokyo she wanted to visit. I applied for jobs in several places and within a week received three job offers. I took up one of the offers in Nagoya, Japan. Had I had a crystal ball or *imbas forosnai*, I would not have gotten on that Asiana airliner. What happened next would have a profound effect on my life for the next fifteen years because the unexpected was about to take place.

In July of 2003, we departed Korea and landed at the Nagoya airport. After we'd grabbed our bags, we entered the waiting area, where a man greeted us. "Howdy, you must be Colleen and Diana. You look exactly like your pictures," said Stanley Webber. "Welcome to Japan." Webber was a typical American that you would find in Asia. He was six-foot-three, lanky, and his head was a little small for his body. The first word that came to mind was "geeky." He grabbed our suitcases and threw them in the back of the school van. On the way to our apartment, he spoke to us as though he'd known us forever. He told us about his wife, Haruka Yamada, and his three daughters, Sara (ten), Jennifer (five), and Maria (two).

Forty-five minutes later we were at our new home. Then a thought occurred to Webber and he took us out around the neighborhood to help us get familiar with the area. "On this side of the street is the red light district, but you don't usually see much because it is hidden from the public. Over here is the 九九(QQ) shop or ninety-nine yen shop, and there are lots of restaurants around." Finally, we were done with our mini tour, and Webber carried our bags into the house for us and said he would pick us up the next day. He left and Diana and I looked at each other. "He seems like a friendly person," I said.

"I get a funny feeling about him," my daughter stated. I did too but didn't want to say anything to her. My gut instinct told me something was not right, but I couldn't quite put my finger on what it was. When we venture into the unknown, these feelings are not out of the ordinary.

Our house was a two-story brick home. It was very clean, well kept, and came with a talking whirlpool bathtub. The first thing I noticed was there was no central heating system much like many of the older homes in South Korea. Also, the houses were very close together, and I could hear my neighbors' muffled voices.

Webber picked us up right on time the next morning. "The school is not too far from your place, about a fifteen-minute walk." When we arrived at the school, I noticed that it looked like a little doll house. It was very tall and narrow. The first floor had a computer room, office, and classroom. The second, a bathroom, a kitchen, and three more classrooms. The third and fourth floors, the owner's residence. There were cameras in every classroom which recorded the teachers. Although the school was small, it had a warm, welcoming feel about it.

The first day at the school, I met the teacher whom I was replacing. James was a tall, young, blond-haired, friendly Canadian. He'd been teaching in Japan for a year with his girlfriend. Interestingly, he told me that his apartment had been broken into twice and all of his electronics stolen. I didn't think much of it, but as time went by, it became significant. I walked by the office and could see a petite Japanese lady answering the phone: "Mushi mushi." We went upstairs and Haruka Yamada followed a few minutes later. "Hello, I am Haruka, the owner of the school. It is nice to meet both you and Diana. How is your house? If there is anything you need, please let us know."

"Hello, Haruka," I said. "The house is fine and it is great to meet you."

Haruka was a thin, petite woman. Her hair was neatly cut into a bob. She was very friendly, and very busy. We didn't have much of a chance to speak to her.

Once the owners had gone downstairs, the Canadian teacher told us that things were not as they appeared here. I glanced over at my daughter and didn't say anymore because Stanley was back upstairs. A second teacher from the USA told us to be careful about what was said in the school. Their comments would remain in the back of my mind, but I didn't think anything of it until later. The first day I spent following around another teacher, watching the school's teaching methods, and then started to teach my own classes the next day.

DISGRUNTLED WORKER AND EXPLOSION

IT WAS THE 18TH of September 2003, a routine day at work and the beginning of my second month at the school. All of the teachers heard a very loud blast in the distance and then the sound of fire engines and police sirens. We later learned that a disgruntled worker had firebombed the Keikyubin Company, killing five and injuring forty-three. I was surprised that there was an element of terrorism even in a quiet country like Japan. The motivation for the attack was money owed to him for the last two months, which he had been unable to collect. Another element of terrorism and very close by.